FURTHER
FOURTH
ASSESSMENT PAPERS IN

ANSWER BOOK
JM BOND

Nelson

Here is a table of bus fares. To find out how much it will cost to go from The Drive to The Peak, find the column headed "The Drive" and look down it until you find the line which says "The Peak". The fare will be 80p.

Kings Road

30	Station Road						
45	30	The Drive					
70	45	30	Church Street				
80	70	45	30	High Street			
85	80	70	45	30	Hill Tor		
90	85	80	70	45	30	The Peak	
95	90	85	80	70	45	30	Bus Station

Find the fares from:

1 Kings Road to Hill Tor 85p

2 Church Street to The Peak 70p

3 High Street to the Bus Station 70p

4 Station Road to the Bus Station 90p

5 The Drive to Hill Tor 70p

6 Kings Road to Church Street 70p

Complete the following sums by filling in the missing signs.

7 $10 \times 5 - 20 = 30$

8 $8 \div 2 \times 4 = 16$

9 $7 + 8 \div 3 = 5$

10 $3 + 4 + 5 = 12$

11 $10 \times 2 - 7 = 13$

12 $10 \times 3 \div 6 = 5$

2

Find two letters which will end the first word and start the second.

13 redu <u>ce</u> ase   14 repe <u>at</u> tempt

15 rais <u>ed</u> itor   16 cere <u>al</u> most

17 rema <u>in</u> side   18 smoo <u>th</u> ink

Underline the correct answers.

19

20

21
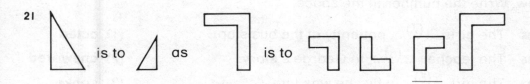

22
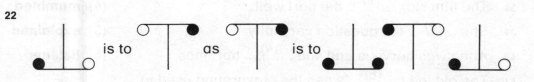

23–26   Can you sort out the jumbled words in the extract below?

After a **dogo** <u>good</u> deal of creeping and **gniwlrac** <u>crawling</u> they peered round the trunks and **odelko** <u>looked</u> into a clearing where some **ester** <u>trees</u> had been felled and the ground levelled.

From *The Hobbit* by J. R. R. Tolkien

3

Here are the names of some pop and rock stars, and the years in which they were born.

Paul Young (British) born 1956
Stevie Wonder (American) born 1950
Bruce Springsteen (American) born 1949
Alison Moyet (British) born 1961
Grace Jones (Jamaican) born 1952
Michael Jackson (American) born 1958

27–28 The oldest of these stars is   Bruce Springsteen
       The youngest is   Alison Moyet

29 In which year did Stevie Wonder have his 30th birthday?   1980

30 In which year was Grace Jones 21 years old?   1973

31 Which is the youngest American listed?   Michael Jackson

32 Which is the youngest British star listed?   Alison Moyet

33 How old will Grace Jones be in the year 2000?   48

34 How old will Michael Jackson be in that year?   42

Use words from the column on the right of the page to complete the lines below. Write the number in the space.

35 The girls ....(7).... patiently at the bus stop.   (1) **acted**

36 The teacher ....(6).... to George's story.   (2) **answered**

37 The girl ....(5).... why she was late.   (3) **spoke**

38 The film star ....(1).... the part well.   (4) **mumbled**

39 She ....(2).... the question very fully.   (5) **explained**

40 Anna was nervous and she ....(4).... her lines.   (6) **listened**

41 The old lady ....(8).... when the playground used to   (7) **waited**
    be a field.

42 I think I ....(3).... to her on the telephone.   (8) **remembered**

Find the word which matches the definition and which also rhymes with the word on the left.

43 **cow**   Part of a tree   bough   44 **raft** A current of air   draught

45 **mile** Part of a church   aisle   46 **rove** A colour   mauve

47 **taste** Part of the body   waist   48 **laws** A short stop   pause

4

Here are some words which have been written in code. Look at them carefully because the code numbers may not be beneath the right words.

tarred	red	read	dare	rated
52769	5629	9256	569	725569

What should be the code for these words?

49	**tarred**	725569	50	**red**	569	51	**read**	5629
52	**dare**	9256	53	**tread**	75629	54	**rated**	52769
55	**date**	9276	56	**rat**	527	57	**art**	257
58	**dear**	9625	59	**tart**	7257	60	**err**	655

Look carefully at this table. It shows the performance of seven makes of computer.

	Keyboard	Display	Memory	Sound	Instructions	Editor	Basic
Plum							
Armitage							
Calculus							
Admiral							
Digical							
Brasilia							
Fleetwood							
Key	Very good	Good	Average	Poor	Very Poor		

61	Which machine was considered best overall?	Digical
62	Which was considered worst overall?	Calculus
63	Which machine got top marks for three features?	Digical
64	Which machine was given the middle mark for five features?	Fleetwood
65	Which was thought to have the worst sound?	Calculus
66	Which was thought to have the best editor?	Brasilia
67	Which was Armitage's best feature?	Keyboard
68	Which was Plum's worst feature?	Memory

5

The twins are having a party on December 30th. Gary's party is three days later, but Cathy is having hers a week before the twins.

69 Gary's party is on *January 2nd*

70 Cathy's party is on *December 23rd*

71 The twins have to postpone their party for a fortnight. It is now on *January 13th*

Here is part of a train timetable.

	Train A	Train B	Train C
Crewe	14.50	16.25	17.22
Alsager	14.59	16.34	17.31
Kidsgrove	15.05	16.41	17.37
Longport	15.11	16.47	17.43
Stoke-on-Trent	15.22	16.53	17.49

72 Which train takes the longest time to travel from Crewe to Stoke? *A*

73 Which train takes the shortest time to do the same journey? *C*

74 Which two adjacent stations would you think are the greatest distance apart? *Crewe and Alsager*

75 Which train takes the longest time to travel between Alsager and Longport? *B*

76 Mr. Bell lives in Crewe, and has to be in Kidsgrove by 5 o'clock. Which train should he catch? *B*

77 How long does it take Train C to travel from Alsager to Stoke? *18 minutes*

78 How long does it take Train A to travel from Crewe to Longport? *21 minutes*

Find a word which can be put in front of all the other words in the line.

79	breeze	side	front	food	*sea*
80	weight	back	mill	clip	*paper*
81	buffalo	colour	fall	heater	*water*
82	box	directory	number	receiver	*telephone*
83	keeper	boat	hold	plant	*house*
84	office	wood	room	number	*box*

One word on each line cannot be formed from the letters of the word on the left (using each letter once only). Underline that word.

85	**statesman**	steam	meant	<u>estate</u>	meats	stamen
86	**corporation**	<u>notice</u>	troop	actor	oration	train
87	**destructive**	truce	divert	strive	cruet	<u>crests</u>
88	**cumbersome**	crumb	member	summer	<u>slumber</u>	score

The words on each line follow a pattern. Look for it and then complete the line.

89	abode	bed	babel	ale	baker	are	bedew	<u>ewe</u>
90	befog	beg	count	cot	dodge	doe	games	<u>gas</u>
91	heard	dear	hover	rove	sober	robe	panel	<u>lane</u>
92	trace	races	wheel	heels	haunt	aunts	graft	<u>rafts</u>
93	diver	die	bairn	bar	fauna	fan	heart	<u>her</u>
94	outer	rut	petal	let	ripen	nip	frame	<u>era</u>

Put these words into alphabetical order.

cushion   **customer**   **culinary**   **culture**   **cupboard**   **curable**

95	Which word comes first?	<u>culinary</u>
96	Which word comes last?	<u>customer</u>
97	Which word comes immediately before **cupboard**?	<u>culture</u>
98	Which word comes immediately after **curable**?	<u>cushion</u>
99	Which word comes immediately after **culture**?	<u>cupboard</u>
100	Which word comes immediately before **cushion**?	<u>curable</u>

7

Paper 2

Fill in the last word in each line of this poem. Line 1 rhymes with line 2, line 3 with line 4, and so on. The list of missing words is on the right of the page.

1   Alone, in silence, at a certain time of <u>night</u>   **be**

2   Listening and looking up from what I am trying to <u>write</u>   **feels**

3   I hear a local train along the valley. "And <u>there</u>   **year**

4   goes the one-fifty," I think to myself; <u>aware</u>   **wheels**

5   that somehow its habitual travelling comforts <u>me</u>   **night**

6   making my world seem safe, homelier, sure to <u>be</u>   **aware**

7   the same tomorrow; or the same, one hopes, next <u>year</u>.   **there**

8   "There's peacetime in that train: one hears it <u>disappear</u>   **write**

9   with needless warning whistle and rail resounding <u>wheels</u>."   **me**

10   That train's quite like an old familiar friend one <u>feels</u>.   **disappear**

Siegfried Sassoon

Here are some important dates in world history.

1837	Victoria becomes queen of Britain
1841	New Zealand becomes a British colony
1842	China yields Hong Kong to Britain.
1848	France becomes a republic
1851	Australian gold rush begins
1854	Crimean War begins
1901	Queen Victoria dies
1997	Hong Kong is to be handed back to China

11   For how many years did Queen Victoria rule?   <u>64 years</u>

12   If Hong Kong is handed back to China in 1997, for how long will it have been ruled by Britain?   <u>155 years</u>

13   The Crimean War began <u>17</u> years after Victoria became queen.

14   The Australian Gold Rush began <u>50</u> years before Victoria died.

15   France became a republic <u>6</u> years before the Crimean War started.

16   In which century did New Zealand become a British colony? <u>19th</u> century

In the following passage some of the words have become jumbled. Write them correctly at the end of the line.

17 The **booftall** team was playing — football

18 a **acthm** in a nearby town. — match

19 They were to **ratlve** there by bus — travel

20 and were to leave their **lubc** — club

21 very early in the **minrong**. — morning

22 The **yourenj** was pleasant, they — journey

23 **own** the match and they all — won

24 **doyneje** themselves. They — enjoyed

25 arrived home **alysef**. — safely

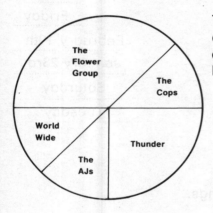

This pie-chart shows how many children like each of five pop groups. There are 48 children altogether.
How many like each group best?

26 The Flower Group — 18

27 World Wide — 6

28 Thunder — 12

29 The Cops — 6

30 The AJs — 6

The world is divided into 24 time zones. When it is midday in London, it is:
2pm in Cairo
9pm in Tokyo
7am in New York
1pm in Rome

31 When it is 10am in New York, what time is it in London? — 3pm

32 When it is 4pm in London, what time is it in Rome? — 5pm

33 When it is midnight in Tokyo, what time is it in Cairo? — 5pm

34 When it is 1am in New York, what time is it in London? — 6am

35 When it is midnight in Tokyo, what time is it in London? — 3pm

36 When it is 6pm in Rome, what time is it in Cairo? — 7pm

Here is the calendar for the first three months of 1993.

1993

	January				February				March				
M	4	11	18	25	1	8	15	22	1	8	15	22	29
T	5	12	19	26	2	9	16	23	2	9	16	23	30
W	6	13	20	27	3	10	17	24	3	10	17	24	31
T	7	14	21	28	4	11	18	25	4	11	18	25	
F	1	8	15	22	29	5	12	19	26	5	12	19	26
S	2	9	16	23	30	6	13	20	27	6	13	20	27
S	3	10	17	24	31	7	14	21	28	7	14	21	28

37 How many days are there in the first three months of 1993? _____90_____

38 If the Spring Term starts on Monday, 4th January and ends
    on Friday, 26th March, how many weeks long is the term? _____12_____

39 The next Leap Year after 1993 will be 1996

40 On what day was Christmas Day 1992? Friday

41 3 weeks after January 29th will be February 19th

42 A fortnight before February 6th will be January 23rd

43 April 3rd 1993 is on a Saturday

44 December 29th 1992 was on a Tuesday

This chart shows the reigns of four Plantagenet kings.

Henry II	1154 – 1189
Richard I	1189 – 1199
John	1199 – 1216
Henry III	1216 – 1272

45 Which king ruled for the longest time? Henry III

46 How long did he reign? 56 years

47 Who ruled for the shortest time? Richard I

48 How long did he reign? 10 years

49 For how much longer did Henry II reign than John? 18 years

50 Thomas-a-Beckett was murdered in 1170. Who was king then? Henry II

51 The first Parliament was held in 1265. In whose reign was this? Henry III

52 For how many years did the Plantagenet kings reign altogether? 118

Fill each space with the number of the answer.

53	A pack of	...(4)...	(1) **furniture**
54	A suit of	...(5)...	(2) **drawers**
55	A suite of	...(1)...	(3) **china**
56	A flight of	...(6)...	(4) **cards**
57	A chest of	...(2)...	(5) **clothes**
58	A set of	...(3)...	(6) **steps**

A rectangular room is three times as long as it is wide. The perimeter is 24 metres.

59 What is the length?   9 metres

60 What is the width?   3 metres

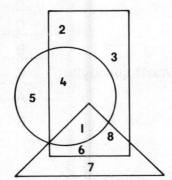

61 Which number is in the circle, the triangle and the rectangle? 1

62–65 Which numbers are in one shape only? 2, 3, 5 and 7

66 Which number is in the circle and the rectangle only? 4

67–68 Which numbers are in the triangle and the rectangle only? 6 and 8

Here is part of a schedule of radio programmes.

9.05 – 10.45	For schools
10.45 – 11.00	Service
11.00 – 11.48	Analysis
11.48 – 12.00	Tales of Long Ago
12.00 – 12.27	You and Yours
12.27 – 1.00	Round Britain Quiz

69 How long does *Tales of Long Ago* last?   12 minutes

70 Which is the longest programme?   *For schools*

71 *Round Britain Quiz* lasts: 33 minutes

72 How much longer is *Analysis* than *You and Yours*?   21 minutes

73 How much shorter is the *Service* than *Round Britain Quiz*?   18 minutes

74 From 9.05am to 1pm is how many minutes?   235 minutes

11

From the letters of the word **transparent** form new words having the following meanings:

75	To peel	pare	76	Not far away	near
77	A weapon	spear	78	Instructions for knitting a jumper	patter
79	Someone who joins in a race	entrant	80	To look with wide open eyes	stare
81	Used up	spent	82	A person with whom one works or plays	partne

Here is part of a train timetable:

	Train A	Train B	Train C
London Paddington	19.30	22.55	23.50
Reading	19.52	23.27	00.24
Bristol	21.04	00.44	01.35

83 Which is the fastest train for the whole journey?   A

84 Which is the second fastest?   C

85 The slowest is   B

86 Which train travels from Reading to Bristol the most quickly?   C

87 Which train is the second quickest?   A

88 The slowest train for this part of the journey is   B

89 **man** is to **woman** as **he** is to she

90 **horse** is to **stable** as **snail** is to shell

91 **man** is to **men** as **goose** is to geese

92 **aunt** is to **uncle** as **niece** is to nephew

93 **north** is to **south** as **smooth** is to rough

94 **drink** is to **thirsty** as **food** is to hungry

One word on each line is different from the others. Underline that word.

95	ascend	climb	lower	elevate	raise
96	see	perceive	look	glance	hear
97	hinder	leave	desert	abandon	forsake
98	timid	shy	nervous	cunning	frightened
99	marched	punched	jogged	walked	ran
100	silly	absurd	ridiculous	comical	swift

12

Paper 3

Find a word which could be put in front of all the words in each line.

1	bank	paper	castle	pit	sand
2	call	table	watcher	bath	bird
3	gloves	ball	band	stamp	rubber
4	worm	case	mark	shelf	book
5	beater	cup	shell	timer	egg
6	bag	shake	basin	cuff	hand
7	ball	rest	bridge	print	foot
8	guard	alarm	bomb	place	fire

If 3 Chewies and 2 Toffs cost £1.40
and 2 Chewies and 2 Toffs cost £1.10

9 What is the cost of I Chewie?   30p

10 I Toff costs   25p

Underline two words on each line which have an association with the word on the left.

11–12	**circle**	square	oblong	round	number	shape
13–14	**piano**	locks	keys	time	notes	letters
15–16	**shoe**	hoof	dress	foot	sole	leg
17–18	**hand**	stop	signal	finger	screw	nail
19–20	**cup**	race	winner	saucer	handle	water

21–26   Which of the following amounts can be made up from three coins?

15p	45p	72p	85p	53p
14p	39p	48p	12p	59p

Below is a chart which shows the populations of the largest English towns (outside London) at different times.

1662		1801		1861	
Norwich	7300	Manchester	84,000	Liverpool	443,900
York	7290	Liverpool	77,600	Manchester	441,100
Bristol	6925	Birmingham	73,600	Birmingham	296,000
Newcastle	5960	Bristol	63,600	Leeds	207,100
Exeter	5290	Leeds	53,100	Bristol	154,000

27-28 Which two pairs of towns reversed their positions from 1801 to 1861?
Manchester and Liverpool/Leeds and Bristol

29 Which town appears in all three lists? Bristol

30 Which town is in the same position in 1801 and 1861? Birmingham

Underline the correct number in the bracket.
31 Bristol was roughly (12, 10, 9, 8, 7, 3) times larger in 1801 than in 1662.

32 Manchester was roughly (2, 3, 4, 5, 6) times larger in 1861 than in 1801.

Can you complete the following expressions? The missing words all begin with the letter **c**.

33 Every cloud has a silver lining
34 A cock and bull story
35 To paddle your own canoe
36 She shed crocodile tears
37 Too many cooks spoil the broth
38 To carry coals to Newcastle
39 To ring the changes
40 To throw cold water on something

Find a word which has both of the meanings given.

41 Not high
Noise made by a cow low

42 A kind of tree
What remains after a fire ash

43 An animal's skin
To conceal oneself hide

44 A piece of ground
A secret plan plot

45 On a lower level
Fine hair or feathers down

46 Noise made by a dog
The outer part of a tree trunk bark

14

One hundred children took an English test. The table below shows their scores.

Score	Number of children
35–39	1
40–44	2
45–49	5
50–54	10
55–59	16
60–64	28
65–69	19
70–74	11
75–79	5
80–84	2
85–90	1

47 How many children gained more than 90 marks?   0

48 How many gained fewer than 40 marks?   1

49 How many gained 75 marks or more?   8

50 Which is the largest group? Those scoring   60–64

51 How many more children gained 75 marks or more, than gained fewer than 45?   5

52 If the pass mark was 50, how many children passed?   92

53 How many children failed?   8

54 A credit mark was given to those scoring 70 or more marks. How many were in this group?   19

On each line, underline the items which are associated with the object named on the left.

55–56 **window**   paper   <u>sill</u>   tint   sun   <u>glass</u>   room

57–58 **jug**   <u>lip</u>   nose   saucer   spoon   <u>handle</u>   rubber

59–60 **door**   flower   paint   <u>handle</u>   green   <u>step</u>   floor

61–62 **chair**   sit   <u>seat</u>   <u>legs</u>   hands   table   floor

63–69 Here is part of a recipe for making shortbread, but some of the verbs have been omitted. There is a list of them below. Can you put them in the right places?

<u>Sieve</u> the flour and the salt into a basin. <u>Cut</u> the butter into pieces and <u>rub</u> it in until the mixture looks like breadcrumbs. <u>Mix</u> in the sugar and knead the mixture until it <u>forms</u> a ball and <u>looks</u> quite smooth. <u>Line</u> a tin with greaseproof paper.

forms   line   sieve   looks   cut   mix   rub

15

70-78 Here is a magic square containing each of the first 16 numbers. All lines, columns and diagonals add up to the same number. The four corner numbers also add up to 34 as do the four numbers in the centre. Fill in the missing numbers.

16	3	2	13
5	10	11	8
9	6	7	12
4	15	14	1

Find the value of each letter in the following sums.

$$
\begin{array}{r} 53 \\ ab \\ \hline 29 \end{array} -
\qquad
\begin{array}{r} 47 \\ c \\ \hline 235 \end{array} \times
\qquad
\begin{array}{r} 147 \\ 3d9 \\ \hline 526 \end{array} +
\qquad
\begin{array}{r} 131 \\ e)\,786 \end{array}
$$

79 $a = 2$ **80** $b = 4$ **81** $c = 5$ **82** $d = 7$ **83** $e = 6$

Think of two letters which will finish the first word and begin the second.

84 amu <u>se</u> ven   **85** spo <u>on</u> ce   **86** bee <u>ch</u> ance

87 pro <u>ve</u> rb   **88** sta <u>ke</u> ep   **89** wed <u>ge</u> ese

90-95 A Prime number is a number which is not divisible by any number except itself and 1. Underline the prime numbers below:

<u>11</u>   15   18   <u>17</u>   4   12   <u>5</u>

6   21   <u>19</u>   9   <u>23</u>   <u>29</u>   30

On each line one word is different from the others. Underline that word.

96 small   little   miniature   tiny   <u>minority</u>

97 uprising   <u>panic</u>   revolt   riot   revolution

98 chubby   fat   <u>tall</u>   plump   stout

99 <u>annoy</u>   astonish   surprise   startle   amaze

100 famous   noted   renowned   <u>popular</u>   well-known

Paper 4

Here is part of a ferry timetable.

Sea crossings from Portsmouth to Jersey

Monday to Thursday

| Depart Portsmouth | 22.15 | Arrive Jersey | 08.20 | the following morning |
| Depart Jersey | 09.40 | Arrive Portsmouth | 18.40 | the same day |

Friday and Sunday

| Depart Portsmouth | 22.15 | Arrive Jersey | 07.00 | the following day |

Saturday

| Depart Jersey | 21.30 | Arrive Portsmouth | 07.15 | the following day |

1 If you travel on a Tuesday, how long does it take to get from Portsmouth to Jersey? .... 10 hours 5 minutes

2 If you travel on a Sunday, how long does the journey take? .... 8 hours 45 minutes

3 The difference in time between the two journeys is: .... 1 hour 20 minutes

4 On a Saturday, travelling from Jersey to Portsmouth takes? .... 9 hours 45 minutes

5 How long does it take on a Wednesday? .... 9 hours

6-9 A number can be divided by 3 if, when the digits of that number are added together, they are divisible by 3.
Example: Is 4578 divisible by 3?
4 + 5 + 7 + 8 = 24
24 is divisible by 3, so 4578 is too.

Underline any of the numbers below that are divisible by 3.

| 575785 | 234567 | 929394 | 777320 |
| 820128 | 907060 | 114455 | 801501 |

Here is part of a train timetable.

| Station | Trains | | | |
	A	B	C	D
Reading	07.25	08.32	11.17	14.00
Reading West	07.28	08.35	11.20	14.03
Theale	07.34	08.41	11.26	14.09
Aldermaston	07.40	08.47	11.32	14.15
Midgham	07.45	08.52	11.37	14.20
Thatcham	07.50	08.57	11.42	14.25
Newbury	07.57	09.04	11.49	14.32

10 Emma lives in Reading. She wants to be in
Newbury by 10am. Which train must she catch?   B

11 How long does it take to travel from Reading
West to Theale?   6 minutes

12 Between which two consecutive stations is
the journey longest?   Thatcham and Newbury

13 The train which leaves Aldermaston at 11.32
arrives at Thatcham at   11.42

14 The train which leaves Midgham at 08.52
arrives in Newbury at   09.04

Fit the words on the right of the page into the poem.

15 I had a hippopotamus; I kept him in a shed   **frolicked**

16 And fed him upon vitamins and vegetable bread   **known**

17 I made him my companion on many cheery walks,   **remark**

18 And had his portrait done by a celebrity in chalks   **kept**

19 His charming eccentricities were known on every side   **made**

20 The creature's popularity was wonderfully wide   **had**

21 He frolicked with the rector in a dozen friendly tussles **was**

22 Who could not but remark upon his hippopotamuscles   **fed**

Menu

Sausages, chips and vegetables	£3.50
Fish, chips and vegetables	£4.20
Ice cream sundae	£1.90
Cheesecake	£1.20
Coca Cola	80p
Service charge	10%

Three friends, Adam, Barry and Chris, went out for a meal. Adam and Barry had sausages and Chris had fish. Adam and Barry had ice cream while Chris had cheesecake. They all had Coca Cola. What was the total cost?

Bill	**£**
Sausages, chips and vegetables	7.00
Fish, chips and vegetables	4.20
Ice cream sundae	3.80
Cheesecake	1.20
Coca Cola	2.40
	18.60
Service charge	1.86
	20.46

Think of a word which can be put in front of all the words on each line.

32	bulletin	cock	forecast	proof	weather
33	cloth	napkin	spoon	tennis	table
34	cream	hockey	skating	cap	ice
35	print	tip	nail	puppet	finger
36	ache	dress	land	light	head
37	work	watcher	tower	golf	clock
38	handed	luggage	over	wing	left

Special Long Weekend Fares

Atlanta	£299	Miami	£339
Baltimore	£349	New York	£299
Boston	£299	Orlando	£349
Chicago	£299	Philadelphia	£319
Dallas	£299	Pittsburgh	£355
Fort Lauderdale	£339	St. Louis	£299
Houston	£289	Tampa	£349
Los Angeles	£329	Washington	£349

Valid for departure from the U.K. any Thursday or Friday; returning the following Sunday or Monday.

39 The cheapest fare is to Houston

40 The most expensive is to Pittsburgh

41 What is the difference between the prices? £66

42 To how many of these places is the fare £299? 6

43 To how many other places is the fare the same as to Fort Lauderdale? 1

44 To how many other places is the fare the same as to Washington? 3

45 What is the difference between the fare to Washington and the fare to New York? £50

Below are some jumbled words. Find out what they are. (They are all connected with holidays.)

46 **chabe** beach   47 **mmigwnsi** swimming   48 **riaptro** airport

49 **vlater** travel   50 **ggglaue** luggage   51 **smage** games

Put each of these words in the correct column.

fork   dollar   chisel   franc   hammer   rake
screwdriver   cent   trowel   rupee   hoe   pliers

	Coins		Garden tools		Carpenter's tools
52	dollar	56	fork	60	chisel
53	franc	57	rake	61	hammer
54	cent	58	trowel	62	screwdriver
55	rupee	59	hoe	63	pliers

Underline the word which rhymes with the word on the left.

64	**yacht**	taught	draught	knot	laugh	caught
65	**heir**	her	fair	hire	tire	weir
66	**front**	mount	font	taunt	hunt	jaunt
67	**sour**	tower	pour	dour	mower	tour
68	**suite**	suit	lute	quite	might	meat

(underlined: knot; fair; hunt; tower; meat)

One pair of words on each line is different from the other two pairs. Underline the odd pair.

69	escape/getaway	remedy/cure	health/sickness
70	circle/square	means/resources	sufficient/enough
71	misery/despair	request/ask	refuse/offer
72	submit/yield	attack/defend	repose/rest
73	guilty/innocent	plan/scheme	sure/certain
74	contradict/agree	require/need	clumsy/awkward
75	cover/conceal	dim/bright	hint/suggestion

(underlined: health/sickness; circle/square; refuse/offer; attack/defend; guilty/innocent; contradict/agree; dim/bright)

The peak rate for telephone calls is charged between 9am and 1pm; the standard rate is charged between 1pm and 6pm, and also between 8am and 9am. The cheap rate is charged between 6pm and 8am. This chart shows the charges (in pence) for calls over a distance of 35 miles, at these rates.

35 MILES +	1 min	3 min	5 min	10 min
Cheap rate	10p	20p	30p	60p
Standard rate	10p	30p	50p	1.00
Peak rate	15p	40p	65p	1.30

76 What is the difference in price between a 5-minute cheap rate call and a 5-minute peak rate call? <u>35p</u>

77 How much cheaper is it to make a 10-minute call at 3pm than at noon? <u>30p</u>

78 How much dearer is a 5-minute call at 5pm than at 7am? <u>20p</u>

79 If I pay 65p for a call at one of these rates, how long will it last? <u>5</u> minutes

80 I would then be charged at <u>peak</u> rate.

81 If I pay 10p for a call, how long is it likely to be? <u>1</u> minute

82 Between which times must this call have been made? <u>1pm and 8am</u>

Here is a histogram which shows the heights of some children.

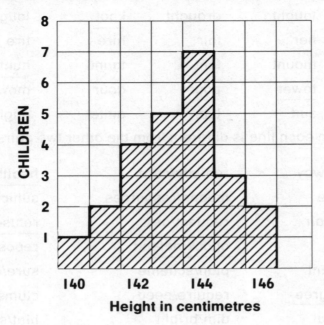

Height in centimetres

83	How many children were measured?	24
84	How many were 143cm tall?	5
85	How many more were 144cm than were 140cm?	6
86	How many were less than 145cm?	19
87	How many were more than 142cm?	17
88	How many were over 146cm?	0

Complete the following chart.

	Train departs	Length of journey	Train arrives
89	10.29	33 minutes	11.02
90	8.24	55 minutes	09.19
91	11.55	1 hour 7 minutes	13.02
92	14.45	22 minutes	15.07
93	20.21	2 hours 47 minutes	23.08
94	23.50	17 minutes	00.07

22

Here are the prices of some holidays in Sorrento in Italy.

	7 nights		14 nights	
	Price per adult	Child under 16	Price per adult	Child under 16
May	£350	£315	£520	£460
June	£400	£360	£600	£530
July	£430	£400	£650	£600
August	£450	£410	£680	£620

95 Find the cost of a holiday for Mr. and Mrs. Reed, and Jane, aged 11, for 2 weeks in June.   £1730

96 What will it cost 2 married couples (no children) to have a week in August?   £1800

97 Mrs. Stephens and her son (aged 8) want a week's holiday in May. What will it cost?   £665

98 My uncle and aunt have saved £550. How much more will they need for a week in July?   £310

99 How much does one adult save by having a week's holiday in May rather than in August?   £100

100 How much less than £1000 will it cost Miss Johnson to have a fortnight's holiday in August?   £320

In a test, Adam, Mark and Paul each gained 69 marks, Sarah and Richard 74, Oliver 38, Jane 81, Elizabeth and James 48, Philip 72 and Stephen 45.

1-9   Complete the list of marks beneath the column graph.

10-20   Show the information given above in the column graph.

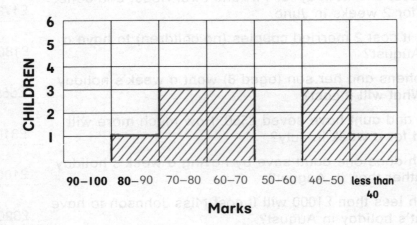

Think of two letters which would finish the first word and start the second.

21   hear th ink   22   stab le ft

23   nie ce nt   24   plea se cure

25   pat ch ink   26   inha le nt

27   blame me ant   28   wor se ems

Look at each pair of words below. If they have the same meaning write **S**; if they are opposite, write **O**.

29   opaque/transparent   O   30   accept/refuse   O

31   verdict/sentence   S   32   senior/junior   O

33   aware/ignorant   O   34   challenge/dare   S

35   question/answer   O   36   commerce/trade   S

37   remedy/cure   S   38   comprehend/understand   S

	Picture quality	Sound stability	Tape wear
SDL Super	▨	□	▨
Singalong	◣	◣	▨
Wayfarer	□	▨	▨
Highspot	▨	▨	▨
SDL Standard	▨	▨	
Toptone	□	■	□
Toptone Extra	□	▨	▨
Supersound	▨	□	□
Supersound 2	▨	▨	▨
Special X	▨	□	▨

Key
- ▨ excellent
- ▨ good
- □ average
- ◣ poor
- ■ very poor

This chart shows how different makes of video tape were rated.

39	Which video had top rating for sound?	SDL Standard
40	Which had top rating for picture quality?	Supersound 2
41	Which had top rating for tape wear?	Wayfarer
42	Which had the lowest rating for sound?	Toptone
43	Which had the second highest rating for all three features?	Highspot
44	How many had the second highest rating for picture quality?	5
45	How many had the second highest rating for sound?	4

46–51 Some words in the following passage have been jumbled. Can you work out what they are?

I could never **mmrreeeb** remember whether the clocks went

dwafrro forward for summer and back for **wirten** winter or vice versa

until a **eifdnr** friend gave me this simple rule: **gripns** spring forward,

fall **kabc** back.

Think of a word which rhymes with the word on the left and also fits the definition.

52 **vain**   A sheet of glass   pane

53 **toy**   Something to which a ship may be moored   buoy

54 **dough**   An enemy   foe

55 **say**   The noise made by a horse   neigh

56 **dam**   A young sheep   lamb

57 **word**   A collection of animals   herd

Each of these words is written in code, but the code is not always placed beneath the right word. Can you sort them out?

ponder	**pound**	**pun**	**pod**	**drone**	**roped**
329	359746	357	76594	65347	35297

58 **ponder** should be 359746   59 **pound** should be 35297

60 **roped** should be 65347   61 **pun** should be 329

62 **pod** should be 357   63 **drone** should be 76594

In the same code write the following words:

64 red 647   65 done 7594   66 none 9594

67 proud 36527   68 prude 36274   69 under 29746

Recipe for Yorkshire Pudding

The instructions have been listed in the wrong order. In each of the spaces provided, write a number to show the correct order.

70 ...(5)...   Beat well

71 ...(7)...   Bake 25–30 minutes in a hot oven

72 ...(2)...   Break in the eggs

73 ...(8)...   It is ready when it is a golden brown colour

74 ...(4)...   Add the milk to make a creamy texture

75 ...(1)...   Sieve the flour and salt into a bowl

76 ...(6)...   Pour into a tin (it must be hot and well greased)

77 ...(3)...   Mix the eggs into the flour mixture

Some words have been omitted from this poem. They are listed on the right of the page. Can you find out where they should go?

78	No sun – no moon!	**street**
79	No morn – no noon	**locomotion**
80–81	No dawn, no dusk – no proper time of day	**go**
82	No sky – no earthly view	**coast**
	No distance looking blue –	**sun**
83	No road – no street, no t'other side of the way	**dawn**
	No end to any row,	**view**
84	No indications where the crescents go	**noon**
	No top to any steeple	**day**
85	No recognitions to any people	**people**
	No courtesies for showing 'em	
	No knowing 'em	
86	No travelling at all – no locomotion	
	No inkling of the way – no notion	
	"NO GO" by land or ocean	
	No mail, no post	
87	No news from any foreign coast	

T. Hood

On each line one word is different from the others. Underline that word.

88	babble	bound	blare	blast	buzz
89	swoop	strut	soar	scamper	squeal
90	sheaf	flock	herd	drove	swarm
91	sow	cock	doe	heifer	duck
92	mare	cygnet	chick	calf	cub
93	oats	wheat	barley	flour	rye
94	creak	crackle	clean	clang	clatter

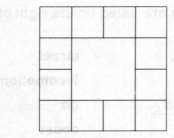

95 The diagram shows that a frame, made out of small squares, and 4 squares wide and 4 squares high contains 12 small squares.

96 How many squares will there be in a frame 5 squares wide and 5 squares high? 16

97 A frame that is 7 squares wide and 7 squares high will contain 24 small squares.

98 A frame that is 9 squares wide and 9 squares high will contain 32 small squares.

99 A frame that is 10 squares wide and 10 squares high will contain 36 small squares.

100 A frame which is made up from 44 small squares will be 12 squares wide and 12 squares high.

Paper 6

This chart shows journey times for cross-channel ferries and hovercraft on various routes.

Route		Time
Portsmouth	– St. Malo	9 hrs
Sheerness	– Flushing	7 hrs
Portsmouth	– Le Havre	5 hrs 30 mins
Southampton	– Cherbourg	5 hrs
Dover	– Zeebrugge	4 hrs 15 mins
Folkestone	– Ostend	4 hrs 15 mins
Newhaven	– Dieppe	4 hrs
Dover	– Dunkirk	2 hrs 20 mins
Ramsgate	– Dunkirk	2 hrs 15 mins
Dover	– Boulogne	1 hr 40 mins
Dover	– Calais	1 hr 15 mins
Dover	– Boulogne	40 mins
Dover	– Calais	35 mins

1   How much longer does it take to cross from Portsmouth to St. Malo than from Portsmouth to Le Havre?   3 hours 30 minutes

2   How much quicker is it to travel from Dover to Boulogne by hovercraft than by ferry?   1 hour

3   How much quicker is it to travel from Dover to Calais by hovercraft than by ferry?   40 minutes

4   How much longer does it take to travel from Dover to Zeebrugge than from Dover to Dunkirk?   1 hour 55 minutes

5   On this chart, which is the only British port to have a hovercraft service?   Dover

6   How many British ports listed have ferry services?   7

What is the name of:

7   A book containing words arranged alphabetically, together with their meanings and pronunciation   dictionary

8   A machine which can store, retrieve and process data   computer

9   A machine used to photograph bones or other parts of the body which cannot be seen otherwise   X-ray

10 A likeness of a person obtained using a camera   photograph

11 Goods which are sent to other countries to be sold   exports

12 Goods which are sent from other countries to be sold here   imports

13–17   A number can be divided by 4 without remainder if the last two digits of the number form a number which is divisible by 4.
Example: 146 is not divisible by 4 as 46 is not a multiple of 4.
184 is divisible by 4 as 84 is a multiple of 4.

Underline any of the following numbers which is divisible by 4 without remainder.

| 3568 | 7777 | 8880 | 2468 | 3434 |
| 8642 | 3546 | 2796 | 3572 | 9198 |

18–21

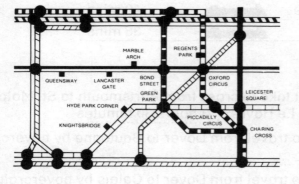

Key

Victoria line
Central line
Circle line
District line
Metropolitan line
Northern line
Bakerloo line
Piccadilly line
Jubilee line

This map shows part of the London Underground system. We want to go as quickly as possible from Regents Park to Marble Arch.

18 On which line is Regents Park?   Bakerloo

19 On which line is Marble Arch?   Central

20 We will change lines at   Oxford Circus

21 Through which station will we pass?   Bond Street

Fill each space with an adjective derived from the word on the left.

22	**circle**	A _circular_ table
23	**marvel**	A _marvellous_ film
24	**continent**	A _continental_ holiday
25	**autumn**	_autumnal_ colours
26	**energy**	An _energetic_ game
27	**centre**	A _central_ location
28	**nation**	A _national_ holiday
29	**quarrel**	A very _quarrelsome_ boy

Vast-Value Superstore announced their seasonal savings as follows:

	Usual price	Sale price
Fresh rump steak (per lb)	£4.10	£3.60
Lean fresh beef mince (per lb)	£1.50	£1.30
Rindless bacon (per lb)	£2.55	£2.28
Dog food (4-can pack)	£2.20	£1.90

30	How much would it cost to buy 2 lbs of rump steak and 2 lbs of mince in the sale?	£9.80
31	How much less is this than the normal price?	£1.40
32	16 cans of dog food in the sale would cost?	£7.60
33	How much less is this than the usual price?	£1.20
34	3 lbs of bacon in the sale would cost	£6.84
35	This is a saving of	81p
36	If I bought 1½ lbs of mince and 2 lbs of bacon in the sale it would cost	£6.51
37	How much less than the usual price is this?	84p

From the letters of the word **tournament**, form other words with these meanings.

38	A friend _mate_	39	To climb _mount_	40	Not wild _tame_
41	Extra _more_	42	A fish _trout_	43	Intended _meant_
44	A special occasion _treat_	45	The study of living things _nature_

31

Anne and Karen play the piano and the violin, Karen and Claire play the violin and the flute, and Anne and David play the clarinet and the piano.

46 How many children play three instruments? 2

47 How many children play the piano? 3

48 Who plays the violin but not the piano? Claire

49 Who plays the clarinet but not the violin? David

50 Which instrument doesn't Anne play? flute

51 Karen doesn't play the clarinet

Fit the words listed in the right-hand column into the poem.

Isabel met an enormous bear; **scream**

52 Isabel, Isabel didn't care **hungry**

53 The bear was hungry, the bear was ravenous, **eat**

54 The bear's big mouth was cruel and cavernous **care**

55 The bear said, "Isabel, glad to meet you **worry**

56 How do, Isabel, now I'll eat you". **cavernous**

57 Isabel, Isabel didn't worry **hands**

58 Isabel didn't scream or scurry **ate**

59 She washed her hands and she straightened her hair up, **meet**

60 Then Isabel quietly ate the bear up.

Ogden Nash

Think of pairs of words which sound alike, but have different spellings and meanings.

61 Part of the foot heel

62 To cure heal

63 A percussion instrument cymbal

64 A sign symbol

65 A tree yew

66 A female sheep ewe

67 A lion's den lair

68 A hen that produces eggs layer

This chart shows the distance (in miles) between Calais and Boulogne and various European destinations.

	Calais	Boulogne
Amsterdam	223	249
Berlin	574	598
Bordeaux	550	506
Brussels	122	146
Cannes	743	712
Cologne	253	269
Copenhagen	661	686
Esbjerg	640	664
Faro	1,393	1,362
Florence	887	850

69 Calais is nearest to: Brussels

70 Boulogne is farthest from: Faro

71 How much further is Cologne from Boulogne than from Calais?   16 miles

72 How much nearer is Bordeaux to Boulogne than to Calais?   44 miles

73 Which town is 640 miles from Calais?   Esbjerg

74 Which town is 850 miles from Boulogne?   Florence

75 How much nearer is Calais to Copenhagen than to Cannes?   82 miles

76 How much nearer is Boulogne to Amsterdam than to Cologne?   20 miles

I was three when my sister was born, and my mother was eight times as old as I was.

77 When I am 20, how old will my mother be?   41

78 When my mother is 50, how old will my sister be?   26

79 When my mother is 50, how old will I be?   29

4 Choc-crisps and 1 Minto cost £1.37
and 4 Choc-crisps and 3 Mintos cost £1.87

80 1 Minto costs 25p

81 1 Choc-crisp costs 28p

33

Here is a chart showing how a class of twenty-four children performed in a test.

Score	Number of children
Under 35	3
35–44	5
45–54	2
55–64	4
65–74	5
75–84	2
85–94	2
95–100	1

82 How many children scored between 85 and 94 marks? 2

83 How many scored 55 or more marks? 14

84 How many scored fewer than 45 marks? 8

85 What fraction of the class was this? $\frac{1}{3}$

86 If the pass mark was 45, how many passed? 16

87 What fraction of the class was this? $\frac{2}{3}$

Complete the following:

88 **dog** is to **paw** as **horse** is to hoof

89 **cat** is to **mouse** as **spider** is to fly

90 **mouth** is to **taste** as **nose** is to smell

91 **toes** are to **foot** as fingers are to **hand**

92 **lion** is to **roar** as elephant is to **trumpet**

Write these numbers to the nearest ten.

93 37 40   94 49 50   95 61 60   96 75 80

97 92 90   98 31 30   99 26 30   100 23 20

34

Paper 7

This chart gives the opening hours of two libraries, **A** and **B**.

	Library A			Library B	
	Hours of opening			Hours of opening	
M	10 – 1	2 – 7.30	**M**	10 – 8	
Tu	10 – 1	2 – 5	**Tu**	10 – 8	
W	CLOSED		**W**	10 – 8	
Th	10 – 1	2 – 7.30	**Th**	CLOSED	
F	10 – 1	2 – 5	**F**	10 – 8	
S	10 – 1	–	**S**	10 – 1	2 – 5

1 For how many more hours is Library **B** open on a Monday than Library **A**? $1\frac{1}{2}$ hours

2 On a Tuesday? 4 hours

3 On a Saturday? 3 hours

4 What is the total number of hours Library **A** is open each week in the mornings? 15

5 For how many hours is Library **A** open in the afternoons each week? 17

6 Library **B** is open for 46 hours each week.

Can you complete the following expressions? The missing words are all the names of living creatures.

7 Put the cart before the   horse

8 Act the   goat

9 Take the   bull   by the horns

10 As blind as a   bat

11 Have a   bee   in your bonnet

12 As proud as a   peacock

13 As happy as a   lark

14 As timid as a   mouse

15 A   fish   out of water

16 One   swallow   doesn't make a summer

This chart shows the heights of some children.

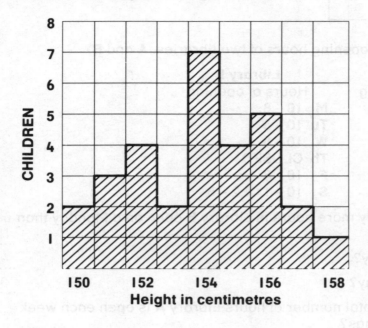

17 What is the difference in height between the tallest and the shortest children? 8cm

18 Which group is the largest? 154cm

19 How many children are this height? 7

20 How many more children are 156cm tall than are 150cm tall? 3

21 How many children were measured? 30

22 How many children are more than 154cm tall? 12

The origin of ink dates back to about 2500 BC, to the peoples of China and Egypt. The early inks were made of lampblack, or soot, mixed with water, vegetable oil or animal glue. As time passed, earth colours were mixed with the other ingredients. Blocks of dry ink are made in the Orient today. Ancient peoples had many other inks for writing and colouring purposes. At one time a secretion from the ink sac of the cuttlefish, for instance, served as a base for ink. Ink was applied to papyrus or paper with a fine-haired brush or a feather. Where clay was used for the writing surface, a sharp, pointed reed was used to impress the letter forms into the clay while it was moist. The clay was dried in the sun or in an oven.

From As things were

23-30 Underline the statements that are true:
People have used ink for over four thousand years

People wrote on paper with a pointed reed
Long ago only black ink was used
Egyptians and Chinese were the first to use ink

The first ink was made by mixing soot with water

Dry ink is made in the Far East today

They wrote on clay with a feather
Instead of water, they sometimes mixed the soot with oil or glue

A sack is carried by some fish
Instead of a fine brush they could use a feather

Ancient people first used coloured ink
Cuttlefish have a pouch inside their bodies

The clay was often dried in the sun

This is part of a coach timetable.

Daily to Bristol

Liverpool	0840
Birkenhead	0855
Rock Ferry	0900
Bromborough Cross	0905
Eastham	0910
Ellesmere Port	0920
Chester	0940
Bristol	1235

31 If you travelled from Liverpool to Bristol, how long would it take? 3 hours 55 minutes

32 How long does it take to go from Birkenhead to Ellesmere Port? 25 minutes

33 How long does the journey from Eastham to Bristol take? 3 hours 25 minutes

34 Between which two consecutive towns does the journey take longest? Chester and Bristol

35-36 Which two places are only five minutes' drive from Rock Ferry? Birkenhead and Bromborough Cross

37

This is a weather chart showing conditions on one particular day.

		°Celsius	°Fahrenheit
Athens	F	20	68
Barcelona	C	19	66
Belfast	C	11	52
Corfu	S	23	73
Florence	C	18	64
Gibraltar	F	22	72
Jersey	C	19	66
Lisbon	R	16	61
London	C	17	63
Luxor	S	39	102
Madrid	F	20	68
Nice	C	18	64
Paris	F	21	70
Rome	F	23	73
Tenerife	R	24	75

F = fair   C = cloud   S = Sun   R = rain

37 How many places are listed as having rain? ......2......

38 Which was the hottest place listed? ......Luxor......

39 What was the temperature there? ......39 °C......

40 This is the same as ......102 °F......

41 What was the temperature in London? ......17 °C......

42 How many degrees hotter was it in Corfu? ......6 °C......

43 24°C is the same as ......75 °F......

44 68°F is the same as ......20 °C......

45 Name another town listed as having the same temperature
    as Athens. ......Madrid......

Here is a family tree.

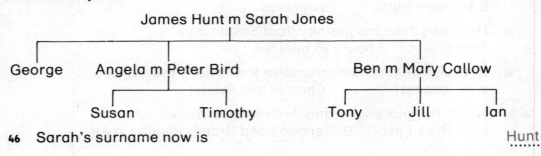

James Hunt m Sarah Jones

George   Angela m Peter Bird   Ben m Mary Callow

        Susan   Timothy   Tony   Jill   Ian

46 Sarah's surname now is ......Hunt......

47	What is Timothy's surname?	Bird
48	What is Jill's surname?	Hunt
49	What is Angela's surname?	Bird
50	Of all the people named on the chart, how many are now called Hunt?	8
51	How many are called Bird?	4
52	What is George's surname?	Hunt
53	How many children did Sarah have?	3

This chart shows the reigns of some British kings.

The House of Lancaster
Henry IV   1399–1413
Henry V   1413–1422
Henry VI   1422–1461

The House of York
Edward IV   1461–1483
Edward V   1483–1483
Richard III   1483–1485

54	Which king reigned for less than one year?	Edward V
55	Which king ruled for the longest time?	Henry VI
56	For how long did he reign?	39 years
57	For how much longer did the House of Lancaster reign than the House of York?	38 years
58	Which king was ruling at the beginning of the fifteenth century?	Henry IV
59	Who was king when the battle of Tewkesbury was fought in 1471?	Edward IV
60	The battle of Agincourt was in 1415. Who was king then?	Henry V
61	The battle of Hexham was in 1464. Who was king then?	Edward IV
62	The Hundred Years War ended in 1453. Who was ruling then?	Henry VI
63	Which Lancastrian king ruled for the shortest time?	Henry V

39

Here is a chart which gives information about Welsh counties. In the spaces, write down the area of each county to the nearest hundred.

	County	County town	Area (sq miles)	Area	Population
64	Clwyd	Mold	837	800	382,500
65	Dyfed	Carmarthen	2,226	2,200	325,600
66	Gwent	Cumbran	531	500	435,600
67	Mid-Glamorgan	Cardiff	393	400	542,000
68	Powys	Llandrindod Wells	1,960	2,000	108,000
69	South Glamorgan	Cardiff	161	200	396,900
70	West Glamorgan	Swansea	315	300	365,000
71	Gwynedd	Caernarvon	1,493	1,500	228,000

72 Which county has the largest population?   Mid-Glamorgan

73 Which has the smallest population?   Powys

74 Which county has the largest area?   Dyfed

75 Which county has the smallest area?   South Glamorgan

76 Which town is the county town of two counties? Cardiff

This grid shows where some children sat in class.

Teacher

5	Lucy		Mark		Michael

(grid positions)

5 Lucy   Mark   Michael
4   Tom
3   Jane
2   Ian
1 Joanne Sarah

   1   2   3   4   5

Give the answers to the following questions in co-ordinates. The number of the column comes before the number of row.

77–78 Where should Charlotte sit if she wants a girl in front of

40

	her and a girl behind her?	2,2
79–80	David wants a boy on either side, so he should sit at	4,5
81–82	Adam wants a boy in front and a boy behind, so he should sit at	5,3
83–84	Gemma would like a boy on one side and a girl on the other, so she should sit at	2,5

This chart shows the temperature for the first week of June in 1985 and 1986.

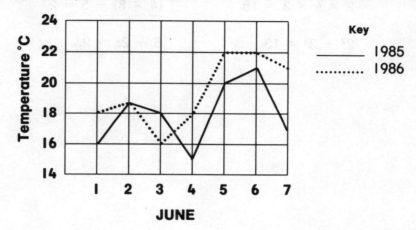

85	On which date was the temperature warmer in 1985 than in 1986?	June 3rd
86	On which two consecutive days in 1986 was the temperature the same?	June 5th and 6th
87	What was the lowest temperature shown in 1985?	15°C
88	What was the highest temperature shown in 1985?	21°C
89	What was the lowest temperature shown in 1986?	16°C
90	What was the highest?	22°C
91	In 1985, on how many days was the temperature lower than 18°C?	3
92	In 1986, on how many days was the temperature above 18°C?	4
93	What was the temperature on June 7th 1985?	17°C
94	What was the temperature on June 7th 1986?	21°C

95-100 Look at the sums below and then underline those whose answers are correct.

$1.0 - 0.25 = 0.75$ $2.5 \times 10 = 2.50$

$\frac{1}{2} + \frac{2}{3} = \frac{2}{5}$ $10^3 = 1000$

$(7 \times 6) + 2 = 44$ $\frac{1}{2} \times \frac{1}{2} \times \frac{1}{2} = \frac{1}{6}$

$2 \times 4 \times 3 = 18$ $(4 \times 8) - 5 = 27$

$2^2 + 3^2 = 13$ $5 - 2\frac{3}{10} = 2\frac{7}{10}$

Paper 8

Find pairs of words which sound the same but are spelt differently, and match the definitions.

1	An animal's nails	claws ⎞	3	Owing	due ⎞
2	Part of a sentence	clause ⎠	4	Moisture	dew ⎠
5	Consumed food	ate ⎞	7	Frozen rain	hail ⎞
6	A number	eight ⎠	8	Healthy	hale ⎠
9	Tresses	hair ⎞	11	Not strong	weak ⎞
10	An animal	hare ⎠	12	A period of time	week ⎠
13	Take dishonestly	steal ⎞	15	Two of a kind	pair ⎞
14	A metal	steel ⎠	16	A fruit	pear ⎠

Find two letters which will end the first word and start the second.

17	che ap pear	18	hab it ch	19	cru el der
20	cho ir ons	21	spo ke rb	22	beg an ts
23	free ze bra	24	du st ray	25	ar ch in

Letter post

Weight	1st class	2nd class
60 g	24 p	18 p
100 g	36 p	28 p
150 g	45 p	34 p
200 g	54 p	41 p
250 g	64 p	49 p
300 g	74 p	58 p
350 g	85 p	66 p
400 g	96 p	75 p
450 g	£1.08	84 p

26 What would be the cost of posting 15 letters (2nd class)? They are all less than 60 g. £2.70

27 How much more would it cost to send 12 letters, each weighing 300 g by 1st class mail instead of 2nd class? £1.92

28 How much less would it cost to send 10 letters, each weighing 450 g 2nd class instead of 1st class? £2.40

29 If I sent one letter of each weight from 60 g to 300 g inclusive by 2nd class mail what would it cost? £2.28

30 If I sent these letters by 1st class mail it would cost £2.97

31 The difference in price is 69p

43

Put each of these words in the most appropriate column.

wrinkled   **twinkling**   **spotty**   **shrill**   **shifty**
short   **oval**   **dyed**   **squeaky**   **straight**   **fat**
sparkling   **deep**   **curly**   **husky**   **closed**

	Voices		Faces		Hair		Eyes
32	shrill	36	fat	40	curly	44	twinkling
33	deep	37	wrinkled	41	straight	45	closed
34	squeaky	38	oval	42	short	46	shifty
35	husky	39	spotty	43	dyed	47	sparkling

This chart shows which holiday resorts may be reached from a number of British airports.

	Gatwick	Luton	Stansted	Heathrow	Exeter	Cardiff	Birmingham	Manchester	Newcastle	Teeside
Tenerife	●	●		●	●	●	●	●	●	
Majorca	●	●	●	●		●	●	●	●	●
Costa Blanca	●	●		●		●	●	●	●	
Costa del Sol	●	●		●	●	●	●	●	●	
Algarve	●	●				●	●	●	●	
Israel	●							●		
Cyprus		●		●			●	●		
Malta	●			●			●	●	●	
Tunisia	●			●				●		

48 Which holiday resort has fewest flights from Britain? Israel

49–50 Which two resorts have most? Costa del Sol and Majorca

51 Which British airport has flights to only one holiday location? Stanstead

44

52 To which holiday location is there no flight from Gatwick? Cyprus

53-54 Which two British airports have flights to only two of these foreign resorts? Exeter and Teeside

DECEMBER

Sun	Mon	Tues	Wed	Thur	Fri	Sat
	1	2	3	4	5	6
7	8	9	10	11	12	13
14	15	16	17	18	19	20
21	22	23	24	25	26	27
28	29	30	31			

55 December 1st is a Monday

56 The last day of December is a Wednesday

57 Christmas Day is on a Thursday

58 Boxing Day is on a Friday

59 Four weeks after December 6th is January 3rd

60 A fortnight before December 14th is November 30th

61 How many Wednesdays are there in this December? 5

62 How many Sundays are there? 4

Complete the following table of television programme times.

		Begins	**Lasts for**	**Ends**
63	**A**	20.25	35 minutes	21.00
64	**B**	19.50	80 minutes	21.10
65	**C**	17.20	45 minutes	18.05
66	**D**	19.40	55 minutes	20.35
67	**E**	15.25	50 minutes	16.15
68	**F**	17.35	95 minutes	19.10

69 What time is $2\frac{1}{2}$ hours before 1.15 pm? 10.45 am

70 What time is $1\frac{1}{4}$ hours after 5.50 am? 7.05 am

71 What time is 50 minutes before 10.25 pm? 9.35 pm

This chart shows the number of books borrowed from Herston Library in one year.

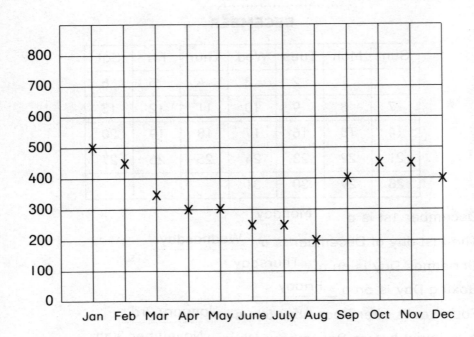

72　In which period were the most books borrowed? (Spring, summer, autumn, <u>winter</u>)

73　In which period were the fewest borrowed? (Spring, <u>summer</u>, autumn, winter)

74　In which month were the most borrowed? <u>January</u>

75　In which month were the fewest borrowed? <u>August</u>

76　How many fewer were borrowed in August than in November? <u>250</u>

77　How many more were borrowed in October than in June? <u>200</u>

78　The number of books borrowed fell in 4 successive months:
(May to August, <u>January to April</u>, March to June,

September to December)

79　Between which two consecutive months was the greatest difference in numbers of books borrowed? (February/March, May/June,
<u>August/September</u>, October/November)

80　How many more were taken out in the first 3 months of the year than in the second 3 months? <u>450</u>

Put a ring round the largest number and underline the smallest:

81–82	5214	5142	5412	5241	(5421)	<u>5124</u>
83–84	(17472)	17247	<u>17127</u>	17274	17227	17142
85–86	98076	<u>98067</u>	98670	(98706)	98087	98607
87–88	59743	59437	59734	59473	<u>59347</u>	(59744)

Complete each expression with a word from the list.

89 Beck and call

91 Bucket and spade

93 Part and parcel

95 Long and short

97 Stuff and nonsense

99 Up and coming

90 High and dry

92 Lock and key

94 Far and away

96 Down and out

98 Fear and trembling

100 Chop and change

away
short
coming
nonsense
call
change
key
dry
out
spade
parcel
trembling

Paper 9

From the letters of the word **compassionate** form new words having the following meanings:

1	We wash with it	soap		
3	The flesh of animals	meat		
5	Part of the face	nose		
7	We see this when the kettle boils	steam		

2	To throw up in the air	toss
4	Useful when eating	spoon
6	Part of the foot	instep
8	To see something	notice

Fill the space in each sentence with one of these conjunctions.

though   **until**   **unless**   **because**   **before**

9   You must not go out _until_ you have written the letter.

10   She put up her umbrella _because_ it had started to rain.

11   The toddler fell over _before_ we could reach him.

12   You will be late for school _unless_ you hurry.

13   We couldn't get our sums right _though_ we did try very hard.

If the words below were spelled backwards, and then put into alphabetical order, in which order would they come? Write a number in each space to denote the order.

(1) plum   (2) pear   (3) apple   (4) apricot   (5) damson   (6) raisin

14   1st (3)   15   2nd (1)   16   3rd (6)   17   4th (5)   18   5th (2)   19   6th (4)

Match the words listed below with their meanings.

20	**avoid**	(3)	(1)	**to express oneself clearly**
21	**asphyxiate**	(4)	(2)	**to make greater**
22	**articulate**	(1)	(3)	**to keep away from**
23	**augment**	(2)	(4)	**to stop a person breathing**
24	**adulterate**	(7)	(5)	**to think about in advance**
25	**abolish**	(8)	(6)	**to achieve**
26	**accomplish**	(6)	(7)	**to make impure**
27	**anticipate**	(5)	(8)	**to do away with**

48

This chart shows the areas of some geographical regions.

Region	Area (km²)
Africa	30.3 million
Asia	26.9 million
Europe	4.9 million
North America	24.3 million
South America	17.9 million
Oceania	22.8 million
USSR	20.5 million

28 Which of these regions has the biggest area? Africa

29–30 North America and Europe are together smaller than Africa.

31 Europe and South America are together exactly equal to Oceania in size.

32 Write the area of Europe in figures. 4,900,000

33 Write the difference between the areas of North and South America in figures. 6,400,000

100 children sat for an examination. The pass mark was 40.

Marks	Number of children
90 or over	7
Between 80 and 89	12
Between 70 and 79	11
Between 60 and 69	20
Between 50 and 59	25
Between 40 and 49	14
Between 30 and 39	8
Under 30	

34 How many children gained fewer than 30 marks?   3

35 How many children failed?   11

36 How many gained 70 or more marks?   30

37 The number of children who gained half marks or more was   75

38 How many children gained fewer than half marks?   25

39 What percentage of the children gained between 60 and 69 marks?   20%

40 What fraction of the children gained between 50 and 59 marks? $\frac{1}{4}$

Use words from the list on the right of the page to complete the poem.

Mrs. Piper, tiny mite,

41 Had a giant's appetite

She, as short as winter grass is,

42 Ate enough for twenty horses

43 No, not even Humpty Dumpty

Had so stretchable a tumpty.

44 She ate so much when food was cheap

45 There wasn't any time to sleep .

46 When food was dear she slept all day

47 Or else, for lack, she pined away

Peter, ere she'd vanished quite

Found a pumpkin for his wife

48 Growing in a field alone;

49 He hollowed it into a home

50 With door and window, leafy shutters

Straw for pipes (in half for gutters)

51 Here they lived, whatever weather

52 Long and happily together

Ian Serrallier

| together |
| shutters |
| growing |
| home |
| appetite |
| here |
| even |
| horses |
| sleep |
| ate |
| food |
| away |

Write these numbers to the nearest hundred.

53 345 300   54 627 600   55 451 500   56 680 700

57 934 900   58 119 100   59 888 900

Underline the word which has a similar meaning to that of the word on the left.

60 **vital**   shape   real   essential   value   weight

61 **unite**   team   together   mix   sort   combine

This chart shows the average daily maximum temperatures in the summer months in London and Ibiza.

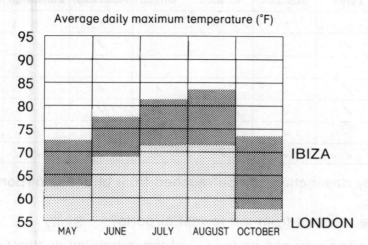

Average daily maximum temperature (°F)

IBIZA

LONDON

62 In which month is the temperature lowest in London?   October

63 In which month is it lowest in Ibiza?   May

64 In which month is there there the biggest difference in the temperatures of the two places?   October

65 In which two months is the temperature the same in London?

July and August

This is part of a train timetable.

Station	Train A	Train B	Train C	Train D
Dorking	07.18	07.22	....	07.40
Box Hill	07.20	....	....	07.42
Leatherhead	07.25	07.28	07.41	07.47
Ashtead	07.28	07.31	07.44	07.50
Epsom	07.33	07.35	07.49	07.55

66 How many of these trains stop at Box Hill?   2

67 How many stop at Ashtead?   4

68 How many start at Dorking?   3

69 Which is the fastest train from Leatherhead to Epsom?   Train B

70 If you wished to travel from Dorking to Epsom which is the fastest train?   Train B

71 Which train starts at Leatherhead?   Train C

51

Here are some details of flights from British airports to holiday destinations.

	Gatwick	Luton	Stansted	Norwich	Bristol	Manchester	Edinburgh	Birmingham
Sicily	✓	–	–	–	–	✓	–	–
Madeira	✓	✓	–	–	–	✓	–	✓
Lanzarotte	✓	–	–	–	–	✓	–	✓
Crete	✓	✓	✓	–	✓	✓	–	✓
Rhodes	✓	✓	✓	–	✓	✓	–	✓
Minorca	✓	–	✓	–	✓	✓	–	✓
Majorca	✓	✓	✓	✓	✓	✓	✓	✓

72   Which holiday destination can be reached from all these airports?
      Majorca

73   Which can be reached from the fewest airports?   Sicily

74   From Birmingham you can fly to 6   of these holiday destinations.

75   Can you fly from Luton to Lanzarotte?   No

76–77   Which British airports have flights to all these destinations?

                   Gatwick and Manchester

78–79   Which British airports have flights to only one of these destinations?

                   Norwich and Edinburgh

From the letters of the word **education** form new words having the following meanings:

80 A dried fruit date   81 A ruling edict

82 A deed action   83 Remarked noted

84 A song for two people duet 85 An amphibian toad

Fill each space with one of the following conjunctions.

although   became   and   but   while   as   when

86 I'm going to the party, but I won't be staying long.

87 I will do some knitting while I listen to the radio.

88 I am staying up to watch the programme although it is very late.

89 The sun is shining and the sky is blue.

90 Will you telephone me when you arrive?

91 Sam put on his gloves because his hands were cold.

92 A lovely smell filled the kitchen as the cake cooked.

93-100   In the following passsage some of the words have become jumbled.
Write them correctly in the space provided.

Dick filled his cap three **smite** times, the horse drinking **linut** until its
burning thirst was quenched, then Dick went up to his **ouedhrsl** shoulder,
patted him, **idnud** undid the line that fastened him, and vaulted
thllgiy lightly on his back. At this unexpected act the horse plunged and
dreare reared a great deal, but Dick stroked him until he
mabece became quiet again, and having done so urged him into a
loplag gallop over the plains.

From *The Dog Crusoe* by R. M. Ballantyne

53

Paper 10

Here are some words which have been written in code. Look carefully at them because the code numbers may not be beneath the right words.

constant	let	notion	cost
7529	159451	839	75129619

What should be the code for these words?

	constant		let		notion		cost
1	75129619	2	839	3	159451	4	7529

Write the words below in the same code

	nets		late		talon		stain
5	1392	6	8693	7	96851	8	29641

	nose		tail		collate		stint
9	1523	10	9648	11	7588693	12	29419

13–20 The following passage is a poem of eight lines. Underline the word which ends each line.

I stood in the gloom of a spacious <u>room</u> where I listened for hours (on and off) to a terrible bore with a beard like a <u>snore</u> and a heavy rectangular <u>cough</u>, who discoursed on the habits of orchids and <u>rabbits</u> and how an electron behaves and a way to cure croup with solidified <u>soup</u> in a pattern of circular <u>waves</u>.

Each of the sets below contains three rhyming words. Some of the letters are missing – can you fill them in?

	sew		**worse**		**home**
21	f^{oe}..	23	n^{urse}....	25	c^{omb}....
22	th^{ough}....	24	v^{erse}....	26	f^{oam}...

	scroll		**bone**		**dim**
27	sh^{oal}...	29	ph^{one}...	31	h^{ymn}....
28	st^{ole}...	30	al^{one}...	32	l^{imb}...

The words on each line follow a pattern. Look for it and then complete each line.

33	silent	slit	praise	pare	frugal	furl
34	alive	evil	merit	tire	redial	laid
35	fatten	fan	vacant	vat	parent	pat
36	parish	pair	custom	cuts	colony	cool
37	derail	liar	credit	tide	depart	trap
38	weary	way	ready	ray	pride	pie
39	music	sum	worth	row	craft	arc
40	shadow	how	spirit	pit	fierce	ice

The answers to the following rhyme with the word on the left, and fit the definitions.

41	**hat**	An insect	gnat	42	**wife**	Used for cutting	knife
43	**raw**	To bite or chew	gnaw	44	**mire**	Group of singers	choir
45	**haze**	Part of a sentence	phrase	46	**list**	Part of the arm	wrist
47	**pot**	Tied in a rope	knot	48	**flew**	A colour	blue

This chart shows the areas and population of some British counties.

County	County town	Area (km²)	Population
Cheshire	Chester	2,328	930,800
Isle of Wight	Newport	381	116,000
Norfolk	Norwich	5,355	689,000
West Midlands	Birmingham	899	2,655,800
Cumbria	Carlisle	6,886	472,000
Suffolk	Ipswich	3,807	602,000
Cornwall	Truro	3,546	422,000

49	Which county has the largest area?	Cumbria
50	Which has the second largest?	Norfolk
51	Which has the smallest area?	Isle of Wight
52	Which has the largest population?	West Midlands
53	Which has the second largest?	Cheshire
54	Which county has a population of over 2½ million?	West Midlands
55	How many counties have a population of over ½ million?	4
56	How many have an area of less than 1000km²?	2

WEATHER GUIDE

	AVERAGE HIGHEST DAY TEMP. °F	AVERAGE HIGHEST DAY TEMP. °F	AVERAGE HOURS OF SUN	AVERAGE HOURS OF SUN
APR	73	56	8	5
MAY	77	58	8	5
JUN	84	68	12	7
JUL	89	71	12	6
AUG	89	70	11	6
SEP	86	66	9	5
OCT	77	57	7	3
	Tunisia	UK	Tunisia	UK

In which 2 months is there the greatest difference in temperature between Tunisia and the UK?

September and October

The least difference in temperature between the two places is in   June

The greatest difference in the hours of sunshine is in

July

The least difference in the hours of sunshine between the two places is in

April and May

63–69   The following passage describes the Duke of York (1763–1827), second son of George III.

He was simply dressed in plain riding costume and was, without exception, one of the finest men England could boast of. He stood above six feet; was rather stout, but well proportioned, his chest broad and his frame muscular; his face bore the stamp of authority, and every feature was handsome; his brow was full and prominent, the eyes greyish, beaming with benevolence; and a noble forehead with premature grey hairs.

Underline the statements below which are correct:

He was a tall man

He wore elaborate riding clothes
He was a leader of men

He did not have much hair
He was sixty-four when he died

It was unusual for him to dress plainly
His eyes were prominent

He had a kind expression

He was a handsome man

He was strong

He lived to be thirty-six years old
His hair turned grey at an early age

Look at the diagram below and then work out the numerical value of the following:

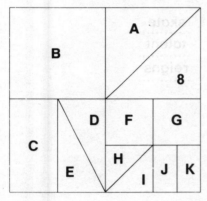

70	The large square (the whole figure)	64
71	The section marked **A**	8
72	The section marked **B**	16
73	The section marked **C**	8
74	The section marked **D**	4
75	The section marked **E**	4
76	The section marked **F**	4
77	The section marked **G**	4
78	The section marked **H**	2
79	The section marked **I**	2
80	The section marked **J**	2
81	The section marked **K**	2

Each of the sets below contains three rhyming words. Some of the letters are missing – can you fill them in?

	laze		**urn**		**site**		**dough**
82	ra _ise_	84	le _arn_	86	he _ight_	88	b _ow_
83	ma _ize_	85	fe _rn_	87	fl _ight_	89	t _oe_

	rum		**mew**		**sort**		**die**
90	th _umb_	92	e _we_	94	th _ought_	96	s _igh_
91	n _umb_	93	q _ueue_	95	c _aught_	97	e _ye_

Write a word which is an anagram of the word on the left and which matches the definition.

98	**steak**	To move across ice	_skate_
99	**latent**	A gift	_talent_
100	**resign**	The monarch does this	_reigns_

Paper 11

This is the calendar for October 1988.

OCTOBER

Mon	3	10	17	24	31
Tues	4	11	18	25	
Wed	5	12	19	26	
Thur	6	13	20	27	
Fri	7	14	21	28	
Sat	1	8	15	22	29
Sun	2	9	16	23	30

1 The last day of October is a .... Monday

2 Three weeks after October 11th is .... November 1st

3 What day is November 4th? .... Friday

4 What day is September 29th? .... Thursday

5 How many days occur five times in October? 3

6 Mum's birthday is the second Tuesday in November.
   What date is it? . ... November 8th

7 A week after October 30th is .... November 6th

8 What was the date of the last Wednesday
   in September? .... September 28th

Put the following words into alphabetical order. Write the number in the space provided.

(1) harbour (2) hard (3) happening (4) harness (5) hatch (6) hanger

9 (6)   10 (3)   11 (1)   12 (2)   13 (4)   14 (5)

Do the same with these.

(1) doesn't   (2) dodge   (3) doctor   (4) donkey   (5) does   (6) dome

15 (3)   16 (2)   17 (5)   18 (1)   19 (6)   20 (4)

My brother is four years older than I am. My mother was seven times as old as my brother when I was born.

21 How old will my mother be when I am 18?   46

22 My brother will then be: 22

23 When my mother is 40, how old will by brother be? 16

24 I will be: 12

25–29 What is the ratio of black squares to white squares? (Answer in the lowest possible terms. For example, 2:1 **not** 20:10)

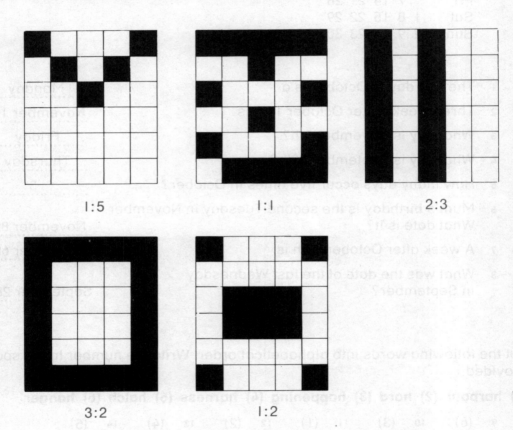

1:5   1:1   2:3

3:2   1:2

30 How many letters in the alphabet are between the second and third vowels?   3

31 How many letters in the alphabet are between the first and fourth vowels?   13

60

	Train 1	Train 2	Train 3	Train 4
Holmhurst	07.12	08.20	....	10.15
Market Town	07.18	....	....	10.21
Brackenbury	07.40	08.40	09.00	10.41
Dinningford	07.50	08.52	09.10	10.51
Stopton	07.58	09.00	09.18	11.00

32 How many of these trains stop at Market Town? ....2.......

33 How many stop at Dinningford? ....4.......

34 How many start at Holmhurst? ....3.......

35 Which is the slowest train from Brackenbury to Dinningford? .....Train 2.....

36 Which is the slowest train from Brackenbury to Stopton? .....Train 2.....

37 Which train starts at Brackenbury? .....Train 3.....

38—45

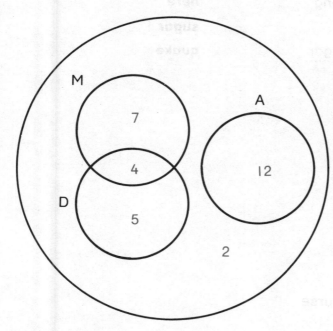

Show the following information about pop groups in this Venn diagram. 30 children were asked their favourite groups. 12 said that they liked the Aztecs only, 7 liked the Merry Men only, 5 liked the Dalmatians only and 4 liked both the Merry Men and the Dalmations. Don't forget to show how many children didn't like any of these groups. Use the letters **A**, **M** and **D** to name your circles.

Fill each space with a word from the list on the right.

46 Precision is a multiplication <u>table</u>

And a railway track,

47 A clock's <u>tick</u>

48 A duck's <u>quack</u>

An iron fence's

Even points

The engineering

49 In our <u>joints</u>

50 The length of <u>time</u>

51 From <u>here</u> to there,

The size of everything

52 We <u>wear</u>

53 The spoonfuls of <u>sugar</u>

In a cake.

The rate of shudder

54 In a <u>quake</u>

Precision loathes

Suppose and guess

Its only words are

55–56 <u>"No"</u> and <u>"Yes"</u>

Its only love

Is old Exact

57 Its only <u>food</u> of course

58 Is <u>Fact</u>

word list
wear
quack
"No"
Fact
table
food
tick
time
joints
"Yes"
here
sugar
quake

Mary O'Neill

Find a word which could be put in front of all the other words on the line.

| 59 | Indian | ink | light | meat | alert | <u>red</u> |
| 60 | box | code | card | woman | age | <u>post</u> |

61	gage	belt	fly	finch	grocer	green
62	air	day	eyed	house	minded	open
63	coat	gauge	bow	forest	water	rain
64	dive	bag	bleed	gay	band	nose
65	lace	band	line	let	tie	neck
66	wood	stick	point	box	maker	match

On each line, one sum has a different answer from the other three sums. Underline that sum.

67	$7 + 8$	$(3 \times 5 \times 1)$	$(2 \times 7) - 1$	$19 - 4$
68	$2 \times 3 \times 3$	$(12 \times 2) - 8$	$36 \div 2$	$(10 \times 2) - 2$
69	$132 \div 11$	$2 \times 3 \times 2$	$(48 \div 4) \times 1$	$(60 \div 12) \times 2$
70	$2 + 3 + 4$	$(4 \times 2 \times 1)$	$56 \div 7$	$(45 \div 5) - 1$

71–76 A number can be divided by 4 without remainder if the last two digits of the number form a number which is divisible by 4.
146 is not divisible by 4 as 46 is not a multiple of 4.
184 is divisible by 4 as 84 is a multiple of 4.

Underline any of the following which is divisible by 4 without remainder.

| 2988 | 4321 | 2998 | 6344 | 9228 |
| 8631 | 7592 | 6335 | 5268 | 6212 |

77–82 Make a magic square using each of the numbers 5 to 13 once only. All the lines, columns and diagonals must add up to the same number.

8	13	6
7	9	11
12	5	10

The ages of my mother and grandmother add up to 93 years. My mother is 25 years younger than my grandmother.

| 83 | My mother is | 34 |
| 84 | My grandmother is | 59 |

Write the following times in the style of the 24-hour clock.

85 5 minutes past midnight   00.05

86 3 minutes past noon   12.03

87 5 minutes before midnight 23.55

88 6 minutes before noon   11.54

The answers to the following are pairs of words which sound the same, but which have different meanings and spellings.

89	The seashore	beach	91	Thick string	cord
90	A tree	beech	92	Notes played together	chord
93	Naked	bare	95	Hair (of animals)	fur
94	A mammal	bear	96	Evergreen tree	fir
97	Guided	led	99	Require	need
98	A metal	lead	100	To work dough	knead

Find a word which could be put in front of all the other words on the line.

1	room	side	sitter	time	stead	bed
2	light	break	dream	nursery	time	day
3	hook	finger	cake	knife	shop	fish
4	gage	fly	light	grocer	house	green
5	brush	grip	style	line	cut	hair
6	cup	bag	cake	pot	towel	tea
7	power	play	shoe	man	trials	horse

The following sentences can all be completed by using the name of an animal or insect.

8 Grandad was very tired so he had a   cat   nap before tea.

9 The knight was very brave; he was   lion   -hearted.

10 Dad knew we were planning to trick him; he said he could smell a   rat.

11 The girl wasn't really sorry; she only shed crocodile tears.

12 He could think of nothing else – he had a   bee   in his bonnet.

13 When interviewed on television, film stars often   fish   for compliments.

14 I'm so hungry that I could eat a   horse.

On each line, find a word which rhymes with the word on the left and fits the definition.

15 **met**   We are in this when we owe something   debt

16 **way**   The noise made by a horse   neigh

17 **poke**   Another name for "people"   folk

18 **pain**   The Queen does this   reign

19 **hymn**   A part of our body   limb

20 **wife**   A piece of cutlery   knife

Distances from UK ports

Distances in miles	Dover	Folkestone
Birmingham	205	198
Cardiff	244	235
Central London	79	71
Edinburgh	457	451
Exeter	248	238
Glasgow	497	491
Leeds	270	268
Manchester	288	281
Newcastle	352	348
Norwich	170	166

Which town and port are farthest apart from each other?
Glasgow and Dover

Which town and port are nearest to each other?
London and Folkestone

What is the difference in mileage between Dover to Manchester and Dover to Edinburgh? ....**169** miles

How much nearer is Glasgow to Folkestone than it is to Dover? ....**6** miles

By how many miles is Folkestone nearer to Norwich than to Exeter?
72 miles

The words on each line follow a pattern. Look for it and then complete the line.

26	amuse	sum	adopt	pod	spire	rip
27	learn	ear	truth	rut	storm	tor
28	heat	the	year	rye	paws	spa
29	stair	rats	trots	sort	plump	pulp
30	matron	man	pulpit	put	sorrow	sow
31	metal	male	merit	mite	chaos	cosh
32	rigid	rid	cheat	cat	haven	hen

Underline the word which rhymes with the word on the left:

33	**caught**	draught	laugh	craft	<u>ought</u>	tough
34	**flower**	pour	<u>sour</u>	grower	mower	poor
35	**tough**	bough	dough	laugh	soft	<u>puff</u>
36	**tongue**	brogue	long	<u>hung</u>	run	dong
37	**goes**	does	<u>woes</u>	lose	loose	noose
38	**fraud**	proud	sound	<u>horde</u>	loud	crowd

39–43 Numbers are divisible by 3 without remainder if the sum of their digits is divisible by 3. Underline the numbers below which are divisible by 3 without remainder.

<u>123456</u>	<u>876543</u>	756776	954259	<u>767643</u>
706040	<u>919191</u>	<u>402204</u>	246842	533666

Complete the poem with words from the column on the right of the page.

Sloppy means: Nothing   **hand**

44 Where your <u>hand</u> can find it. **mind**

And sloppiness   **dress**

45 Is not to <u>mind</u> it. **sash**

46 Run-down <u>shoes</u>, **mess**

Tipped-over trash, **work**

47 Half-done <u>lessons</u>, **shoes**

48 Untied <u>sash</u>,   **dishes**

49 Dirty <u>neck</u> and **torn**

50 Unwashed <u>dishes</u>, **lessons**

Living on a lot   **too**

Of wishes.   **window**

51 <u>Window</u> curtain **neck**

52 <u>Torn</u> and flapping,

53 Little <u>work</u> and

54 <u>Too</u> much napping.

Dresser drawers

55 An awful <u>mess</u>,

Dribbles on a

56 Party <u>dress</u>.

What Sloppy leads to,

You can guess

    Mary O'Neill

This chart shows the reigns of some British monarchs.

House of Hanover

George I	1714–1727
George II	1727–1760
George III	1760–1820
George IV	1820–1830
William IV	1830–1837
Victoria	1837–1901

57 The Great Exhibition was held in 1851.
In whose reign was it?   Victoria

58 In 1769, work began on the Leeds to Liverpool canal.
In whose reign was this?   George III

59 Which Hanoverian monarch ruled for the longest time?   Victoria

60 London streets were first lit by gas in 1814.
Who was reigning then?   George III

61 In 1863 the Co-op was first formed.
Who was on the throne then?   Victoria

62 The Liverpool to Manchester railway used steam power
in 1828. This was in the reign of: George IV

63 For how long did the Hanoverian monarchs rule altogether? 187 years

64 Which of these monarchs ruled for the shortest time?   William IV

65 The first iron bridge was built at Ironbridge in 1788. How
many years was this after George III came to the throne?   28 years

66 Who was reigning when the new London Bridge was
finished in 1827?   George IV

This is a calendar for November 1993.

NOVEMBER

Sun	Mon	Tues	Wed	Thur	Fri	Sat
	1	2	3	4	5	6
7	8	9	10	11	12	13
14	15	16	17	18	19	20
21	22	23	24	25	26	27
28	29	30				

67	Four weeks after November 3rd is	December 1st
68	A fortnight before November 18th is	November 4th
69	What day is October 31st?	Sunday
70	The date of the first Friday in December is	December 3rd
71	A fortnight after November 20th is	December 4th
72	Three weeks after November 5th is	November 26th
73	A week after November 30th is	December 7th
74	A fortnight after October 31st is	November 14th

Put these words into alphabetical order. Write the number in the space.

(1) **dispute**   (2) **discount**   (3) **discuss**   (4) **dishonour**   (5) **disable**

| 75 | 1st (5) | 76 | 2nd (2) | 77 | 3rd (3) | 78 | 4th (4) | 79 | 5th (1) |

Here is part of a train timetable.

Blackpool	0630	London Euston	1645
Poulton	0637	Watford	1701
Kirkham	0648	Crewe	1841
Preston	0709	Warrington	1904
Wigan	0723	Wigan	1916
Warrington	0736	Preston	1933
Crewe	0804	Kirkham	1954
Watford	0940	Poulton	2005
London Euston	▼ 1002	Blackpool	▼ 2016

80	The journey from Blackpool to London takes:	3 hours 32 minutes
81	The return journey takes:	3 hours 31 minutes
82	How long does it take to travel from Crewe to London?	1 hours 58 minutes
83	The return journey takes:	1 hours 56 minutes
84	How long does it take to travel from Preston to London?	2 hours 53 minutes
85	Between which two consecutive stations is the journey shortest?	Blackpool to Poulton
86	Between which two consecutive stations is the journey longest?	Crew to Watford

30 children gave their opinion on some pop groups. This is what they said:

7 liked the Acrobatiks only
6 liked the Big Boys only
5 liked the Cuckoos only
2 liked both the Acrobatiks and the Big Boys
3 liked both the Big Boys and the Cuckoos
4 liked both the Acrobatiks and the Cuckoos
1 liked all three groups

The remainder didn't like any of the groups.

87–94 Show this information in the Venn diagram.

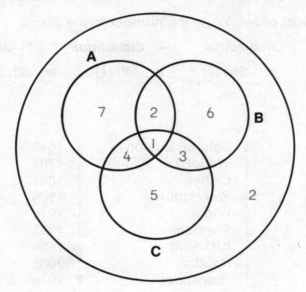

Complete the table below.

	Train departs	Length of journey	Train arrives
95	10.48	28 minutes	11.16
96	11.33	37 minutes	12.10
97	16.51	19 minutes	17.10
98	22.30	46 minutes	23.16
99	10.32	29 minutes	11.01
100	13.53	1 hour 27 minutes	15.20

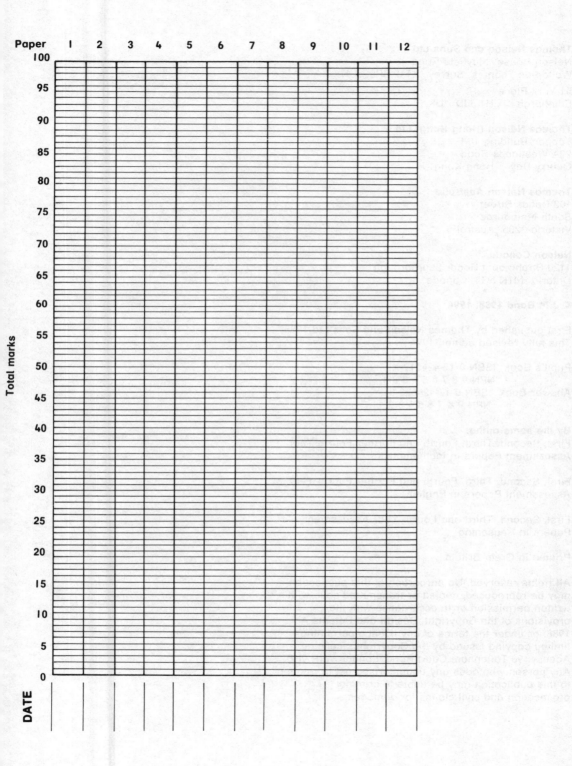

Paper | 1 | 2 | 3 | 4 | 5 | 6 | 7 | 8 | 9 | 10 | 11 | 12

Total marks: 100, 95, 90, 85, 80, 75, 70, 65, 60, 55, 50, 45, 40, 35, 30, 25, 20, 15, 10, 5, 0

DATE

Thomas Nelson and Sons Ltd
Nelson House Mayfield Road
Walton-on-Thames Surrey KT12 5PL   UK

51 York Place
Edinburgh   EH1 3JD   UK

Thomas Nelson (Hong Kong) Ltd
Toppan Building 10/F
22A Westlands Road
Quarry Bay   Hong Kong

Thomas Nelson Australia
102 Dodds Street
South Melbourne
Victoria 3205 Australia

Nelson Canada
1120 Birchmount Road Scarborough
Ontario M1K 5G4 Canada

First published by Thomas Nelson and Sons Ltd 1988
This fully revised edition 1994

Pupil's Book ISBN 0-17-424519-X
            NPN 9 8 7 6 5 4 3 2 1
Answer Book ISBN 0-17-424520-3
            NPN 9 8 7 6 5 4 3 2 1

By the same author
First, Second, Third, Fourth and Further Fourth Year
Assessment Papers in Mathematics

First, Second, Third, Fourth and Further Fourth Year
Assessment Papers in English

First, Second, Third and Fourth Year Assessment
Papers in Reasoning

Printed in Great Britain